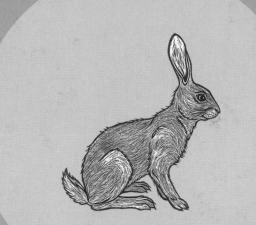

To my parents, for filling my childhood with art and nature. AL x

First published in North America in 2016 by Boxer Books Limited.
www.boxerbooks.com

Boxer® is a registered trademark of Boxer Books Limited.

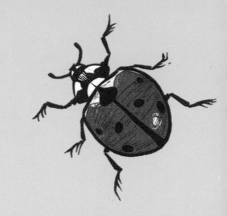

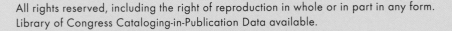

The illustrations were prepared using lino cuts and litho printing with digital color.
The text is set in Futura.

ISBN 978-1-910716-11-3

1 3 5 7 9 10 8 6 4 2

Printed in China

All of our papers are sourced from managed forests and renewable resources.

How Much Does a Ladybug Weigh?

Alison Limentani

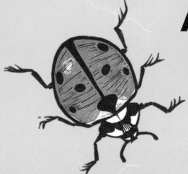

Boxer Books

10 ants
weigh the same as

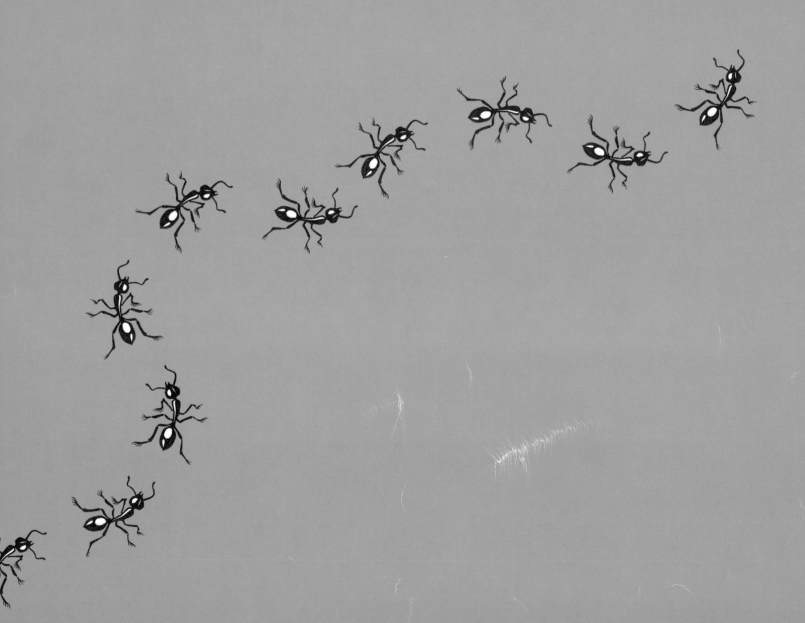

9 ladybugs
weigh the same as

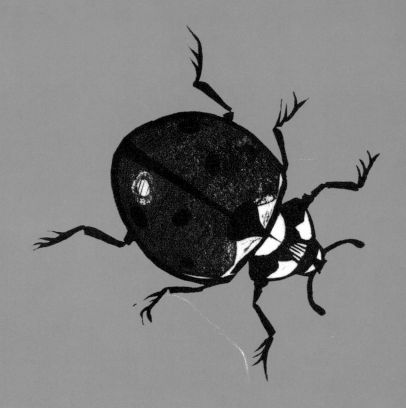

1 ladybug

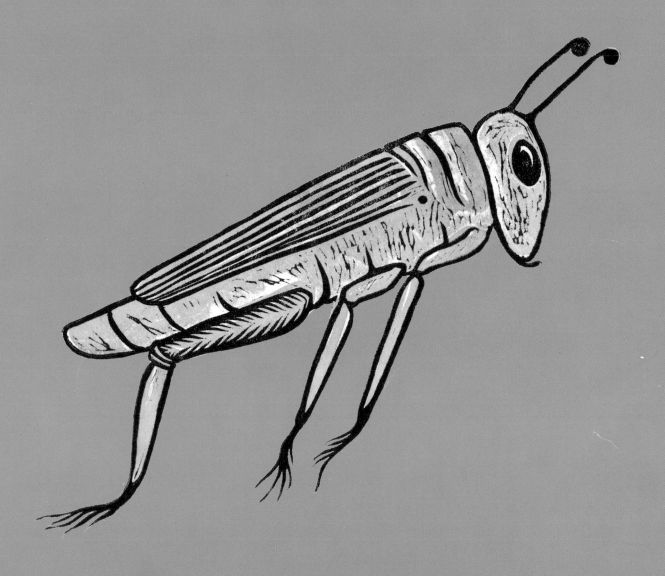

1 grasshopper

8 grasshoppers weigh the same as

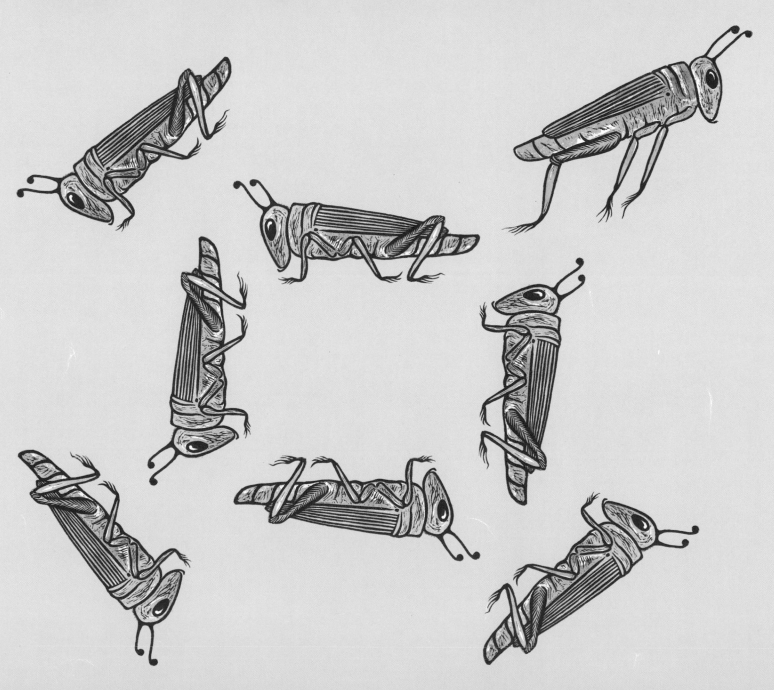

1 stickleback fish

7 stickleback fish weigh the same as

1 garden snail

6 garden snails
weigh the same as

1 starling

5 starlings

weigh the same as

1 gray squirrel

4 gray squirrels weigh the same as

1 rabbit

3 rabbits
weigh the same as

1 fox cub

2 fox cubs

weigh the same as

1 swan

1 swan weighs the same as

ladybugs

ant

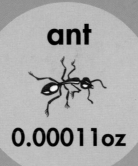

0.00011 oz

ladybug

0.0011 oz

grasshopper

0.0095 oz

Different animals of the same species can vary in weight, just as different people do. All the weights in this book are based on animals within the average healthy weight range.

stickleback fish

0.076 oz

garden snail

0.53 oz

starling

3.2 oz